From Under The Dress

A PLAYWRIGHT BY
MYRA L. TURNAGE

FULL CIRCLE PUBLISHING
BILOXI, MS

Full Circle Publishing
PO Box 8549
Biloxi, MS 39535

For information address Full Circle Publishing Rights Department, PO Box 8549, Biloxi, MS 39535

Editing by Full Circle Publishing & Julie Keene
Manufactured in the United States of America

ISBN-13: 978-0692899472 (Full Circle Publishing)
ISBN-10: 0692899472

www.juliekeene.com

~

A tribute to our forefathers and mothers who built the bridge for all that would dare cross over into freedom. Crossing over the Jordan would be freedom for the mind, spirit, and soul of those who dared not to be bound. We give thanks to those who had the courage and faith to pass through the parted sea into the land of milk and honey. Now... taste and see.

~

SCENE I – *The Kidnapping*

Reminiscent of a young African Prince, strolling along an African riverbank, we see this young man searching for precious stones. This is a daily activity and pastime of the children of village Chiefs. Unexpectedly, the Prince is captured by a rival tribe and rendered unconscious.

SCENE II – *In the Belly of a Portuguese Ship*

Finding himself shackled in the belly of a Portuguese slave ship, our young Prince is among a mass of humanity in the cargo bay. Men, women, and children are chained together so closely that any movement causes friction that leads to ulcerated skin and blisters.

The stench of feces and rotten flesh circulates the air. Many escape to unconsciousness and death.

The gnashing of teeth is only paralleled by the wailing and moans aggravated by stomach hunger pains while rats nibble at exposed fingers and toes. The young Princes' mind wonders in turmoil while being tossed to and fro. He thinks, "No doubt my parents shall rescue me and my people." He ponders, "Why have I been cast out of EDEN into the very debts of HELL?"

SCENE III – *Carolina Harbour* *(St. Sullivan Island)*

It has taken nearly 2 ½ months to cross the Atlantic Ocean – over two months of fear, pain, suffering, disease, and death. For certain, our young Princes' parents have counted him dead. From Africa's interior, his minds ear can hear his mother crying out for him. He wonders what the future holds for him. Are his many hopes and dreams now dead? Is this the end?

SCENE IV – *Rice Plantation*

Safely into his manhood, however still longing for his homeland. He is now an accomplished coachman for his master considering its details, strikingly regal in his black uniform with top hat. He gazes out into the rice and cotton fields. The visions of his parents and village begin to haunt him. Through the thousands of miles that separate them, he could see his mother with her hands above her brow, searching the horizon for her beloved long lost son. Standing beside her is his father. Although his body is strong and firm, tears have formed tracks of sadness that cannot hide the everlasting pain that give way to symbols of loss. From this greatness, his destiny was deterred. What was now to be his future?
STILL WATERS RUN DEEP YES THEY DO!

MONOLOGUE

What of my parents? Do their hearts still long for me? Am I still in their dreams as they are in mine? My father, how he must yearn to see the fruit of his seed. He stood as a mighty tree which gave shelter and provided nourishment to all about him. Oh how his chest expanded when his eyes were upon me. And my mother, the keeper of my soul, loved to teach me the ways of the elders. What a magnificent woman she was. She would be proud of the man I have become.

Will all of my past be as ghosts to me? Shall I shed my past and submit to my master? Can my memories and my new state of being co-exist? I say no! For the greatness that is within me will not allow me to live in bondage. I must rise! I must be free! My children must not be born into this bondage. Their songs shall not be as the song of the caged bird but as the song of the bird of paradise and the whippoorwill which roost and nest in the branches of the tall tree. Their mother shall have free range and scope in her sojourn through motherhood. She will be a pillar of strength and love and the host of a great nation. Her wisdom and determination shall be legendary and inspirational. The seed planted in her fertile soil shall sprout and rise up as mountains. Just as my mother's belly did rise to shelter me, so will my seed rise out of this would be demise. The spirit of my father and my mother will guide and keep me. There is no obstacle strong enough to deter their prayers. Nothing can defeat their hopes. This seed that bears fruit of itself shall RISE!

Ms. M: So what was the most compelling reason you decided to have "THE BALL"?

Ms. O: ....

As Bennett stands on the upper end of the porch extending from the mansion he straightens his top hat and tie. He looks down at the shine on his shoes. He knows the other slaves are looking on with envy as he awaits his master for the ride into town.

Bennett: The lookings of a beautiful day. Yup, a beautiful day.

Bennett can see the little white children so carefully dressed, so befitting a Sunday evening. The laughter and gaiety echoes in his ears while in the distance of his imagination he can hear the laughter of his baby brother whom he so long ago left behind. Baby brother is now a grown man. The sobs of his mother now, at most, only a mournful sigh. But the cries of the slave children are close and plentiful as they resound from the fields and mingle with the laughter of the nearby plantation children. The combination of joy and pain echoes a confusion of sweetness like unto a violin.

Bennett: Someday I will be able to put joy and pain in the same bucket. And on that same day I will be able to separate sunshine from rain and receive my rainbow.

Bennett's heart aches at the thought that his seed may never be passed on as he is forbidden to take a slave girl of the fields and Master has kept the house girls for himself and other plantation owners.

Voice: Someday we'll be together, yes we will, yes we will!

Gracie Mae walks to the edge of the porch. Her golden locks appear to be on fire from the sun. Her emerald eyes are starring at Bennett as though she is trying to penetrate his very thoughts.

Gracie Mae: Hi ya doin' Bennett?

Bennett: Just gettin' ready for town (*his thoughts are on the children of the fields*). Will they ever enjoy such freedom?

Gracie Mae: What did you say Bennett? Oh yonder comes Harriett.

Harriett one of the little slave girls from the fields has wandered into the open yard which is but a playground for Master's children. Although Harriett is a darky from the fields, Gracie Mae has declared her as her most beloved playmate. No adult onlooker would deprive Gracie Mae from her happiness. Harriett with much confidence runs to Gracie Mae...

Harriett: Tag you're it!

Bennett: What a site *(Bennett ponders over the thought that such love and devotion that Gracie Mae and Harriett share has to someday end).*

Bennett: What a site *(Could this friendship last into adulthood or for the rest of their lives?).*

Voice: I have a dream someday**...**

The children run and play without a care. Suddenly, in unison, Gracie Mae and Harriett stop and stare as they watch Bennett usher the men onto the coach for their ride into town. Bennett sits tall and upright as he directs the horses:

Bennett: Gitty up! Gitty up!

The girls admire Bennett's strength and grace.

Harriett: *(Looking at Gracie Mae)* Why is Bennett the only one on the plantation that knows how to Gitty up the horses?

Of course Gracie Mae does not answer her friend

Gracie Mae: Tag you're it

The girls continue their playing.

Ms. M: (*Asks M.O to*) *read the following*: **UNCOLOR ME**

November 26, 2009

Dear President Obama,

　　Today is Thanksgiving Day. I hope you, your family, friends and loved ones are continually blessed. I am writing to you to share a poem with you that I was inspired with a few weeks before the Presidential election. On election night I was at a gathering along with hundreds waiting for the results to come in. I thought about reading this poem to a few people. However, this was one moment I knew everyone in my presence was proud to be a Black American. Intuitively, I reserved. I believe now is the right time to send this to you. I also believe that God's words will not return to him void. I would like to dedicate this to you as President of the United States of America. I also hope that it will be a blessing to you for the rest of your life.

　　When I was standing in the Mall on Inauguration Day, my toes were cold, my nose and feet were freezing. I could barely feel my own hands. I whispered to a few people standing near me, "What if we were homeless and in the cold like this every day?" To my surprise, people started to cry with compassion. I looked at the many multicolored faces all around. The one color that stood out was the color of Love. Later, along with Dr. Lowery, as we recited the Lord's

Prayer, I felt overwhelmed. I felt the scripture cry out.

"If my people who are called by my name, should humble themselves, and pray , and seek my face, and turn from their wicked ways, then I shall hear from my Father who is in Heaven and forgive their sins and heal the land." I knew then that we had begun to heal. Thank **YOU** for all that you are doing and continue to do every day (2nd Chronicles 7:14).

Sincerely

Myra L. Turnage

Ms. O: UNCOLOR ME................................

Uncolor Me

WITHOUT THIS COLOR
WHAT WOULD I BE?
WITHOUT THIS COLOR
WHAT WOULD YOU SEE?
WITHOUT THIS COLOR
LOVE WOULD PREVAIL
FOR LOVE IS THE COLOR
THAT NEVER FAILS
WITHOUT THIS COLOR
WHAT WOULD I BE?
THROUGH LOVING EYES
YOU HAVE THE POWER
TO UNCOLOR ME.
WITHOUT THIS COLOR
WHAT WOULD YOU SEE?
LOVE IS THE COLOR
THAT CAN SET US FREE
LET'S OPEN OUR HEARTS
AND UNCOLOR WE

Ms. M: Do you think even then Gracie Mae had not yet placed a color on her dear friend Harriett?

Ms. O:.....................................

The girls are still at play upon Bennett's return. The men folk are not with him, just Bennett. The girls run up to him knowing as usual he has a treat for them. For Gracie Mae, a large rainbow colored lollipop. For Harriett, two cubes of pure cane sugar. Harriet knows the sugar cubes have been taken from the kitchen food supply on the back of the coach, but loves her treat just the same. Harriett pops one of the sweet cubes in her mouth and puts the other one in her pocket.

Harriett: Sugar cube...ummmm

The girls tarry along behind Bennett as he dismounts and puts away the horses.

Harriett: Bennett what do you do when you go to town? What is town? Where is town?

Bennett: Town is 'bout ten mile down yonder. In town there be cafes, and shops and markets, and cotton gins and a whole bunch of stuff. The men folk go to town for business. The women and children go to town to shop for clothes and sit in on shows and whatever they want to do.

Gracie Mae: Everybody knows what town is. *(Without waiting for any more conversation, she skips away towards the mansion because it is getting late in the evening.)*

Bennett: *(Looking at Harriett)* You better be getting' along home too.

Harriett: There any Nigras in town 'cepting the ones that know how to gitty up horses?

Not waiting for an answer, Harriett scurries along down the hill toward the slave quarters.

Ms. O: I truly believe our ancestor's spirits have inspired such songs as...

In its entirety we hear...

For a moment we can see the beautiful black butterfly being forced by the pressure of the raging African waterfall that propels it on a journey that eyes had never seen nor ears ever heard. Silhouettes of Alvin Ailey dancers wearing graceful bodies and black silk scarfs show themselves. These embodiments are joined by adolescent slave girls all dressed in white, their bodies dance in unison just like a cool summer breeze dances with the sun. They all become one beautiful vapor that pours themselves onto the cotton bows where they temporarily make their home. They know that someday they will again rise.

Voice: Black butterfly sail across the water......

Harriett reaches home. Once inside she rushes towards her mommy hugging her and slipping her the second now soggy and melting sugar cube from her pocket. Mommy smiles and pops the "sugger" into her mouth, feeling the love and desiring the touch of Bennet's sweet lips.

Mommy: *(whispers to herself)* Bennett, my sweet Bennett

Mommy (known around the yard as Elnora) nestles her babies - Harriett, Viola, Peanut (Peter), Lil' Boy (Patrick), the twins Pauline and Paulette, Sandra Fay and Jamie Lee altogether among the hay filled burlap sacks that she has made for their bed. As the children sleep Mommy begins to pray.

Elnora: Heavenly Father, Father God, please cover over all my children and all the children of the fields. Lord, I don't want to pray a selfish prayer. So please, Father God, bless all the Masters and they households too. And Lord, when Master come with the whip and the lynchin' forgive him for this evil for he is ignorant of the hell that awaits all evil. Father, deliver us up like you did the children of Israel. AMEN.

Elnora knows as long as Master's plantation is covered; everything on it is covered.

The mild winds blow through the trees. The wind seems to whisper to the minds of the sleeping slaves, giving them direction and guidance. Elnora can hear the call between the leaves of the trees. The call of the whippoorwill. Elnora knows this is not the sound of the whippoorwill. It is the call of her Bennett. He has come in the still of the night for his beloved Elnora.

Elnora and Bennett sit under the open window. Bennett's head laying in Elnora's bosoms.

Bennett: The voices in my head haunt me. The voices of my far away people. I can see and hear the cries of the African slaves blowing in the wind. Their stories beat in my mind. They are the stories of grandparents repeating the journey from Africa to this place. Elnora we must keep on telling the story.

Ms. O. I believe the spirits of our ancestors are still alive today setting sound tracks for the children of today. Where did this creativity and need for expression come from?

Bennett: What do you think home is like? I mean Africa now a days?

Elnora: *(a beam of light shines down on the couple as Elnora holds Bennett close to her heart)* When I think of home I think of a place with green grass growin'...When I think of homeeee...!

Elnora and Bennett awaken to a burning wicker lamp in their faces. Master got wind of the two and caught them together. Master gives Bennett a lash with his whip.

Master: I ought to have the two of you strung up, right here, right now. Bennett if my blood wasn't running through your veins I would kill you, right here, right now. I just still might. Bennett I hope you kissed your beloved good bye because you won't be seeing her ever again. The two of you better pray don't no darky baby come outta you Elnora. It will be better off if the cord choke it while it's still in your belly. Any darkie neck will be cut no sooner than it comes outta you.

(Bennett thinking to himself) So all the slave gossip is true. Master is my daddy and so it seems all of Elnora's babies is too.

Even though their hearts were breaking, they didn't dare challenge Master.

Only two days had passed since Master caught Elnora and Bennett together.

Elnora: Harriett, I need you and the rest of the children to hear this sad news. The widow Thompson, has taken ill to her death bed. Master is sending me to tend to her for the rest of the time she has left on this earth.

Harriett: So Master punishing you? I will go with you. Or let me go in your place. Your babies need you here.

Elnora: You know Gracie may would never let you leave her. Harriett, you the Momma of this family from now on. My babies now your babies.

(Elnora bowed her head and prayed) Father

God...............

Elnora: Harriett, always make sure to get your dress ready at night. Keep the children fed. Keep yourself healthy and strong. Before long all of you will be old enough to work in the fields. You need to be strong to pick cotton and rice all day.

Elnora goes to the shelf and pulls down the big brown dress. She turns it inside out.

Elnora: Now get your dress ready at night. Pin tight inside your "Holy Bible". You want to keep close to God.

Put in some pain pills to hand out to the slaves. They need it for aching backs from pulling the cotton sacks and the beatings. Keep some empty bottles to sneak to the young "Wet Nannies". When Master's babies be suckling, momma can steal a little and save for her own baby. Keep an empty sock just in case you find a penny on the ground or if you decide to keep a nickel or two of Master's change when you mend his pockets. You can give it to Bennett for when he go to town. Master won't miss it. Of course keep for yourself two cigars and a flask of moonshine for whenst you just can't take no more of them white folks and just about had enough. Take a smoke and drank yourself some. "JUST DON'T EVER LET NOBODY KNOW WHAT'S UP UNDER YOUR DRESS". YOUR LIFE IS UNDER YOUR DRESS. DON'T

NEVER FORGET THAT HARRIETT. YOUR LIFE IS UNDER YOUR DRESS...YOUR LIFE AND YOUR FUTURE.

From Elnora's heart we hear: "If I could, I would protect you from the sadness in your eyes. Give you courage in a world of compromise. Yes I would. If I could, I would teach you all the things I never learned.

And I'd help you cross the bridges that I've burned. Yes

I would...if I could. I would try to shield your innocence from time. But the part of life I gave you isn't mine. I watched you grow now I have to let you go. If I could I would help you make it through the hungry years. But I know I can never cry your tears, babe. But I would if I could. In a time and place where you don't want to be, you don't have to walk this road with me. My yesterday don't have to be your way. If I knew I would change this world I brought you to. Now there isn't much more I can do. But I would if I could. (Regina Bell)

Elnora got her stuff and walked out. The Thompson plantation was about 20 miles down the road. Elnora started walking.

We heard that the widow Thompson died a few months later but Elnora never returned to live on the plantation with her family. Bennett continued to be nice to Harriet and the rest of the children. From time to time Harriett would see Bennett when she came up to play with Gracie Mae. Her time with Gracie Mae was getting shorter and shorter. This saddened Gracie Mae and Harriett and Bennett.

Gracie Mae: *(After a few weeks Gracie Mae went down to the slave quarters to find her friend. It was almost as if Harriett knew Gracie Mae was coming. Bennett was with her)* Harriett I love you and you will always be my favorite of all friends.

Harriett: I believe you mean the words you say.

Bennett: Gracie Mae you have a place. Harriett you have a place. Keep that place deep, deep inside your hearts. The day gone come when you will need to find this place.

Ms. O: I believe that when our ancestors were in the fields working, praying, singing, dancing, protecting Masters' stuff, in spite of their troubles they had faith that someday along would come Mary McCloud, Marian Anderson, Martin, Malcolm, Dorothy and Lena, Vanessa and Halle, Sidney and Denzel, Colin and Barak, Sasha and Malia, Venus, Serena, and Oprah, Dorothy Height, and so many greats. They were coming to "US" for "US". They would rescue and reclaim the land. Our people are our dreams.

VOICE: I know there gonna come a time when my babies won't have to cry in the sun. They won't go hungry while I breast feed Master's baby. I know some day this land I'm toiling will be filled with my seed. From my seed nothing will be withheld. They walked across the Red Sea on to dry land. They came out of the wilderness. They walked Selma. They marched Washington. They stood in the mall and watched Barak inaugurated. We can never make the mistake of standing still when there is a need to move.

We can see the African dancers prepare for the celebratory festivities. Their garb are so full of color. Their movement is so full of energy. It is breathtaking. Can't you hear the power of their voices in the wind and feel the earth trembling to the beat of the drums????? Their voices were so powerful it shook two branches from the lynching tree that stood in the cotton field. The noose snapped and fell to the ground.

DOWN IN THE FIELDS

Viola, Peanut, Lil' boy and the twins start dancing in the fields. They were dancing just like they could hear the songs and beat of the drums coming straight out of Africa. They finished up their ritual.

Viola*:* Peanut, go get that noose! Put it back least Master be the wiser.

Peanut hurried over to the big oak tree and tied the noose up high and tight.

Viola*:* You old African King hush this wind and behave.

The wind ceased as it carried away eight leaves from the big oak tree, eight leaves that represented Elnora's eight babies

Voice*:* Little Children go where I send thee.

Viola: Behave

Gracie Mae: (*Excited as she runs down to the fields*) I need you to come to town with me!

Harriett: (*All the field hands are looking at Harriett with envy, knowing that she is Gracie Mae's best friend and can get out of work just like that*) We have a lot of cotton to get out before the sun go down.

Gracie Mae: Oh come on! Let Peanut and Viola take up your slack. I know you want to get out of this blazing hot sun anyway, don't you? Let's go to town!

Harriett: (*The thought of going to town for the first time made Harriett excited and afraid since she had no reason to go to town for her own self*) What I need in town for?

Gracie Mae: I have lots to show you.

Harriet took the cotton sack strap from around her neck, handed her load to Viola and hurried out of the field behind Gracie Mae.

The girls scurried past all the slave quarters, up the hill towards the mansion. Bennett was waiting for them.

Bennett assists the teenagers onto the coach.

Bennett: You ladies ready for a fun day?

Cindy: (*Yea Cindy*) Girls just wanna have fun, oh girls just wanna have fun, that's all they really want

Gracie Mae*:* Yes Bennett, yes we are. (*Gracie Mae pulls a bonnet from behind Bennett's seat and hands it to Harriett)* Wear this whenever we go to town.

Harriett*: (No questions asked, removed the dust filled rag from her head and put on the bonnet*) Nice bonnet.

The group arrive in town. Bennett helps Gracie Mae down and motions to Harriett that it is ok for her to get off the coach. Bennett secures the horses.

Bennett: How long Gracie Mae?

Gracie Mae: We will meet you right back here in two hours.

Bennett: (*Walks over to Harriett*) Now you need to walk two steps behind Gracie Mae at all times. She will let you know when to stand side by side equal to her. Don't forget two steps behind unlessen she show you otherwise.

Harriett: (*Stomping her feet two times on the ground*) Is that about two steps?

The girls laugh and walk away. Harriett slows down, knowing exactly where her place is.

Bennett: Harriett, I pray your friend see fit to it to keep you safe wise you in town.

Gracie Mae: Harriett we don't do much laughing and talking while we are in town. We just walk and look at things. I will buy things that I need.

After much visiting many stores Gracie Mae heads for the fabric store.
Gracie Mae: Harriett this is my favorite. I saved it for last. Look at all the beautiful fabric.

Harriett could not speak. She walked from aisle to aisle. The beautiful colors and textures were unbelievable to her. In her mind's eye the African Queens made themselves known. They were prancing and dancing and worshipping with their daughters as they prepared them for womanhood. The frocks, the head dress, the jewels were so rich and beautiful. In the midst of all the queens stood LATIFAH and LATIFAY. One was dressed in gold silk, the other in red lace. The majesty of the two overtook Harriett. She knew she must get to where they are. As the bronzed beauties reached for her!!!!!!!!!!!!! COME!

Gracie Mae*:* Harriett, come over here by me. Don't go getting into trouble the first time you come to town.

A group of ladies noticed one of the men inappropriately admiring Harriett. The ladies dared not confront him but confronts Gracie Mae instead.

Lady #1*:* You know you make the slaves have thoughts they ought not have when you bring them to places like this. You need to keep them gathering mercantile and the like. Nigras shouldn't be in here. They might start to think they are as good as we are.

Lady #2: Matilda, you know you have nothing to worry about. Our men would never look at a slave when they have us.

Lady #3: (*Knowing that her husband has fathered more than twenty slave babies speaks up*) Judith, you don't know what's UNDER THAT DRESS!

Gracie Mae: Ladies, please pardon me. My father and mother are having the Spring Ball in a couple of weeks. Harriett is helping me gather a few things for my gown.

Lady #1: You are Spalding Thompson's daughter. My, we do hope to see you there.

Embarrassed and not wanting to get in trouble, the ladies hurry about their own affairs

Gracie Mae completes her shopping. Harriett gathers up the merchandise. They leave to meet Bennett.

Soon they are back on the plantation.

Gracie Mae*:* Bennett, take me down to the quarters first before I go home.

Of course Bennett follows instructions. He stops the coach and is surprised to see Gracie Mae getting down and taking the fabric as well.

Bennett*:* You need help? Harriett can help you. Harriett and Gracie Mae, get the fabrics.

Gracie Mae leads the way inside. The rest have not yet made it home from the fields.

Harriett: You leaving your beautiful thangs down here in this place?

Gracie Mae*:* I know it will be safe here. I want to decide first what I want to wear to THE BALL before my mother decides for me. I am fourteen years old and I have never chosen my own dress. Not even once.

Harriett: All this beautiful fabric you can have a store full of dresses.

Gracie Mae: I'll decide on which fabric first then I will show my mother. It's going to be a hard decision. They all are so amazing.

Bennett: (*Comes up to the door*) Young lady, it's getting late. I best be getting you home.

Just as they are leaving, the others come in from the fields.

Viola is amazed at what she sees.

Viola: My! What is all this about?

Harriett: Gracie Mae needs a ball gown to wear in a couple of weeks.

Viola walks over to Gracie Mae. She puts her hands around Gracie's waist, turns her around, and measures her shoulders.

Viola: Harriett, stand next to Gracie Mae. *(She compares their height)*

Harriett: (*Speaking to her friend*) Vi likes to make dolls for the girls.

Harriett shows off some dolls Vi has made from a worn out baseball and burlap.

Viola*:* I love making beautiful things. I also made cotton sacks for all of us.

Bennett: Yup, it's time to get you home.

Voice: "Somewhere over the rainbow blue birds do fly, why can't I?"

TWO NIGHTS LATER

Harriett and Viola sneak up to the mansion.

Harriett: Vi, you wait here. I will go up and ask to speak with Gracie Mae. It would be bad if they catch you up here. But you are the only one that knows how to measure up Gracie Mae.

Harriet knocks on the door. One of the servant slaves answers.

Slave: Harriett it is late for you to be coming up. The family is settled for the night.

While Harriett states her case, Vi is standing near the back porch. She can hear voices coming through an open window. Out of curiosity and not knowing the real danger she is in, she looks through the open window. No one is familiar to her except Master. There is one young man writing on a chalk board. The household is taking inventory of their slaves and all their property which is common for this time of year. All this is foreign to Viola. She does hear the young man as he writes and names.

Young Man*:* THE CHILDREN OF ELNORA: Viola he says (*as he writes VI…. Vi is stunned as she hears and sees her name*)

Viola: Ah!

For fear of being discovered she jumps down and hides under the porch)

Harriett explains to Gracie Mae why she has come up to the mansion so late in the evening.

Harriett: Vi wants to get started on your ball dress right away. She will have only a few hours in the mornings before she goes to the fields but not much time at night since this is high cotton picking time and the fields hands have to work straight up to dark. Vi is outside waiting to measure you up with me.

Gracie Mae: *(Steps just outside the door)* Vi, Viola where are you?

Viola comes up to the two girls. Stands them side by side. Amazed at how their stature is almost identical.

Viola: Gracie Mae, I will have you dressed up to be the most beautiful girl at the ball.

Gracie Mae: Remember this is our secret for now.

Harriett and Viola hurry themselves down the hill to safety.

For the next couple of weeks, Vi gets up early way before day sewing on dresses for Gracie Mae. Not just one, but a Red one, a Green one, a Yellow one, a Blue one, and a Purple one. They were all so beautiful and grand fit for a queen. As Harriett looked at the beauty, she began to remember the stories that Bennett and momma Elnora told them about African Queens and Princesses. The familiar sounds of chanting haunted her ears while the visions of beauty fellowshipped in sisterly love.

Voice: NUM, NUM, NUM, NUM............ *(Soon the chanting was taken over by the stranger)*

Voice: YOU'RE ONCE, TWICE, THREE TIMES A

LADY AND I LOVE YOU.

Although his voice was new to Harriett she knew in her heart he adored these beautiful Queens

Gracie Mae and Harriet started going to town more and more often. Gracie told Harriett that Master said she needed to learn some business because one day her husband would need her help. Gracie made sure Harriett understood learning business was not a woman's job and no white man would want a wife who knew business but Master had a plan for Gracie. Harriett kept this secret in her heart.

On the next trip to town Harriett noticed white men passing out papers and talking kind to Nigras.

Gracie: *(Warning Harriett)* Those men just trouble makers. Stay far away from them. They ain't no friend of this town. They want to take Nigras away from us.

Harriett I don't want you to leave my family ever.

THREE WEEKS LATER

Gracie comes down to the slave quarters, excited and nervous, excited because Loraine Despeaux has arrived from France and will be staying on the plantation for the next few weeks. Its political business, Gracie explains to the slaves. She is also nervous because the ball is in two days.

Gracie: "I need to see my dress", she informs Harriett and Vi.

Harriett: (*Sends the rest of the house to go outside*)

Go, whise we conduct business in private.

Vi happy to ablidge, pulls back the sheet that unveils gown after beautiful gown. Gracie is shocked

Gracie: My God, Vi! You did all this!

Vi could only smile with love and pride.

Harriett: You must try them on, each and every one.

Gracie*:* Yes! Oh, yes! With pleasure.

While trying on the dresses Gracie notices the letters VI stitched in the hem of each gown.

Gracie*:* Vi why is VI in all the hems?

Vi: That's my name, VI.

Gracie*:* Who told you VI is your name?

Vi*:* I saw the young man write "VI" and say Viola.

Gracie: Vi, don't you ever let any white folk or even

Bennett see you write or say that is your name. If you do, you will have to say goodbye to everyone you love, perhaps goodbye to the world after suffering your punishment.

Vi: Yessum

Gracie: Your name is safe under my dress. I am so happy! I wish I could reward you with something good! Maybe I will take you to town on our next trip.

Vi: Teach me how to read. Teach me to read. That would be good enough for me if I could read.

Gracie: (*Looking at the hunger in Vi's eyes she knew some day Vi would read.*) Viola

A soft wind came through the window picking up a remnant of fabric and draped itself around Vi's neck like a banner. Yes a banner of pride, hope, freedom and victory. In her mind's eye, she could see the smile on the face of Vanessa Williams as she received a jeweled baton from one of the Great Queens of Africa.

Voices: NUM NUM NUM NUM NUM

Gracie: I will have Bennett pick up the gowns

tomorrow. Vi, reading? Maybe you need to just stick to making beautiful dresses.

Vi: How do you spell red, if this dress is red, how do I know that? I just want to read RED. And read my sister and brother name. I know that might put me on my death bed.

THE NIGHT OF THE BALL

Gracie walks in to the parlor where her mother and Loraine Despeaux were socializing and discussing the grand "BALL". The ladies were stunned to see Gracie so elegantly dressed in her beautiful emerald green gown.

Marguerette: *(Gracie's mother)* Darling how fabulous! (*Not knowing what else to say*)

Loraine Despeaux: My, what a vision of beauty! Who is your tailor?

Gracie: There are more. I can show you more.

Gracie so graciously modeled each beautiful gown.

Loraine Despeaux: I will take the purple one. Name your price.

Marguerette*: (Although confused)* The blue one for

me.

She had no idea where her daughter had gotten these amazing gowns.

Loraine Despeaux: I must meet your tailor before I leave. Male or female? (*Before Gracie or her mother could speak, Ms. Despeaux turned up the hem of one gown to discover VI.*) No. 6 how clever!

Gracie: Oh that's just VI's. *(She thinks.......)*

Marguerette*:* Yes, my daughter Gracie is quite the seamstress. She designed and tailored all these beautiful gowns. I want her to be as well rounded in home duties as her father wants her to be in business.

Ms. Marg knows if there is the least evidence that one of her slaves knows anything about reading or writing her family would face legal and social ridicule and Viola would face lynching.

LATER THAT EVENING

The socialites of the town were enjoying an evening of feasting, dancing, and laughing.

The slave servants could hear the festivities through the walls. Some were overcome with sadness and began to have ill feelings for their masters. Before these feelings became any stronger they were rescued by...

Patti*:* "If only you knew how much I do, I do love you. If only you knew how much I do, I do need you." *(Stay strong bring me forth.)*

Marguerette, assuming this strange voice must have come from somewhere in the Ball Room, went to investigate. She saw nothing unusual so she returned to the slave servant quarters.

Marguerette, to her surprise and bewilderment, thought she saw a Nigra slave wearing the exact gown she was wearing leave the Ball Room and head for the slave servant quarters.

Marguerette*:* This can't be possible. *(She followed the slave.)*

Once in the slave servant quarters, Marguerette saw a beautiful Nigra woman dressed identical to herself. All the slaves were dressed in white, both men and women. Their jewelry and head garb were unbelievable and breathtaking to Ms. Marg.

Marguerette: *(walks over to this stranger)* What is this? *(Making reference to her gown and behavior)*

Woman: *(Singing)...“This is LOVE”*

Marguerette: *(Having an out of body experience lets down her beautiful red hair and sings)* “I want to know what love is. I want you to show me. I wanna feel, I wanna feel what love is.”

Woman: This is love, feeling free, walking, and head to the sky, praising HIM.

Marguerette: Show me your love.

Woman: It's all about Love. Marg, take my hand. Dance. Stomp your feet. If he's in your heart, there you will find love.

This queen and all the slaves show Ms. Marg a real good time.

Marguerette and Woman: It's all about Love.

Marguerette straightens herself, returns to her body, takes a big drink and rejoins the socialites.

TWO DAYS LATER

Loraine Despeaux: Marguerette, I would like to take a gown back for my daughter on tomorrow.

Marguerette*: I'm sure that won't be a problem. Which one would you like? I will inform Gracie.

Loraine Despeaux: Oh, not one of these. My daughter is turning sixteen. I would like soft pink for her birthday celebration.

Marguerette: *(Trying to hold her composure)* I will inform Gracie.

Later that evening Loraine Despeaux overhears Gracie giving instructions to Bennett to go into town for soft pink fabric. Gracie also instructs Bennett to inform Vi not to write her name in the hem of the dress.

After dinner Loraine Despeaux asks Marguerette:

Loraine Despeaux: Will the gown be ready for travel on tomorrow?

Marguerette: I am sure.

Loraine Despeaux: Who is Vi and why is she WRITING her name in the hem of Gracie's gowns?

Marguerette knows that she and her daughter have been found out and are at the mercy of Ms. Despeaux. Her worry is how she is going to avoid punishment for teaching a slave to write. What will happen to herself and her daughter and? The punishment for Viola will surely be lynching.

Marguerette: I am at your mercy. How can I convince you to spare the punishment of myself and my daughter, the ridicule of my family and the life of my young slave girl?

Loraine Despeaux: So VI is short for Viola, not the number 6? I think the best way to spare all involved is to send Viola/Vi/VI/No. 6 back to France with me.

The next morning Bennett gathered Viola and the dolls she had made for herself when she was a little girl. Viola hugged her sister Harriett and whispered into her ear. She didn't dare cry but went along with Ms. Loraine Despeaux to town so they could take the train to New York where they would depart for France.

Of course the family was too hurt to react, but knew the option was much more painful. They took comfort in knowing that Viola would be alive in France making beautiful gowns for the proud women there. Where is France? Is it as far away as Africa?

THREE MONTHS LATER

Gracie Mae made her way to the slave quarters. She heard that Harriett had taken to her bed sick.

Missing the companionship of her friend and worried for her health, she had to come calling.

Gracie: *(Shocked at what she was seeing, Harriett's belly was great with child)* Harriett, what have you gone and done? Father will surely send you away when he takes note of this situation. And the darkey field hand will surely be hanged.

Harriett: Gracie, I could never begin to explain my situation to you *(knowing this was Master's baby in her belly)*. I must request of you to honor me with one thing in life which you owe that debt to my beloved Viola. TEACH ME TO READ. As a woman of honor which I believe you are, TEACH ME TO READ while my longsuffering for Vi will not be in vain.

During the next several trips to town Gracie Mae instructed Bennett to pull over to a secret place where she could steal away time and teach Harriett to read. Harriett was a quick learner and soon realized there were white people who wanted to free the slaves. Gracie Mae knew the danger this could bring to herself as well as her family. Harriett's invitations to town ended. Although, now that Harriett had learned that the Abolitionist were helping Nigras escape to freedom she could not stay away from town.

The next trip to town Harriett found a way to hide

underneath the wagon and survive the danger of the travel. As soon as Bennett hitched the wagon and the men were out of sight, Harriett would hurry into the feed store where only slave hands and a few disguised Abolitionist would gather. Harriett learned as much information as she could regarding the road to freedom. The song of the Whippoorwill became the song of freedom.

Voice: Is my living in vain? Is my giving in vain? Is my praying in vain? Oh no! Of course not! Cause up the road is eternal gain!

After praying on her knees, in the still of the night Harriett pulled the burlap bag from under her bed. She put on the beautiful red gown Vi had left especially for her. Remembering the whisper of Vi's voice.

Vi: The red is for blood of protection.

Viola began to lace up the corset in the back of the dress. Each lattice represented the stripes from the whip.

Vi: Always remember "by his stripes we are healed".

Viola faded away into the safety of Harriet' heart.

Harriett removed the gown and lay in bed and placed the beautiful gown over herself for a COVERING. In the wee hours of the morning Harriett awakened to find herself in a puddle of blood flowing from her womb.

A FEW WEEKS LATER

In the middle of the day from out of nowhere Josephine came running, screaming and yelling for Harriett.

Josephine: Harriett, I know you the only one can help me. Please help me, Harriett. My babies done come. Twin boys done come. They darkies! They throats as good as cut! When Master find out I marked his kin or house Nigras, my babies as good as dead! Please help me Harriett!

Harriett: Fetch me them babies along with your birthing rags then send for Bennett. Make no wiser to anyone what has went on here. When the twins got there Harriett lay herself in bed and placed the babies at her bosoms.

Bennett: (*Rushes to Harriett's side.*) I am happy to see you have brought more to love into this world. I will shelter them as my own. We will wait the seven days for their color to set in then we will let Master know his plantation still growing some more.

Before sunrise Harriett got up and nursed her babies. Once their bellies were full and coated she gave them both asfidity and karagoric. She made sure they had enough to keep them for at least four hours. Once the babies were good and still, Harriett placed them inside half cut cotton sacks, making sure they could breathe, she strapped them to her flat belly and met Bennett who was all ready to head into town. Strangely enough, neither Bennett nor Gracie Mae questioned Harriett. When they reached town, Gracie being use to Harriett's duties did not question her as she went straight to the grain and feed store. Gracie went to socialize in the café.

Just as Harriett had prayed, one of the Abolitionist was waiting for her. She gave him written instructions. She also told him where he could place information for as well as find her information on the horses and on the buggy. She made him well aware that her trips to town would be few and far between. She took the babies FROM UNDER HER DRESS, kissed her beloved babies and handed them over to the white man.

Abolitionist: You are a good and brave woman.

Harriett: Just promise me this...Jacob and Isaac will reach the Promised Land.

Voice: Precious Lord take my hand. Lead me on. Let me stand. Take my hand Precious Lord and lead me on. (Donny McClurkin**)**

Harriett requested from the abolitionist two bags of water well tied. She wrapped the bags of water in Josephine's bloody birthing rags, strapped them to her belly then gathered one bag of feed and met Bennett at the buggy.

Once they were well outside of town Harriett's water broke. She went into labor. She demanded Bennett stop the buggy.

Gracie Mae: Good Lord Harriett! Didn't you know you were too far along to be coming into town?

Do you know how to birth your own baby?

Bennett escorted Harriett off the buggy and onto the ground a few feet away from the buggy, sparing Gracie Mae. The stillborn babies were delivered. Bennett got a shovel off the buggy and dug a shallow grave. He buried the babies along with Harriett's secret.

Bennett: I suppose I should keep the birthing rags for show when I give Master the bad news. He was looking forward to growing his plantation with babies from his best girl.

Gracie Mae cried the rest of the way home. She had always been able to feel Harriett's pain. She could also feel her thoughts and emotions. She knew her beloved Harriett had gone through something only a woman of strength, faith, courage, and most of all love could. She longed to have a heart like her friend.

After this ordeal Gracie Mae began keeping a journal.

In it she expressed her displeasure of how women (white women of course) were being treated as second class citizens. She also spoke out (in private of course) her feeling of slavery in the South. While she did not understand why White men were taking slave girls to bed producing mixed breeds while many white women craved to have babies but were forbade only to have as few as necessary to aire the family. She was also confused by her own compassion, perhaps love even for the Nigras.

Gracie Mae: I do not understand my love hate relationship. Sometimes I feel like I love the Nigras and hate my Family.

BLESSED HARVEST

Fall was coming. This was a special time of year. The hot smothering summer was over. Families from out of town came to visit. Some even came from out of state and out of the country. One evening Gracie Mae was in town, she saw a tall handsome bronzed man with beautiful curly hair. She was told he was visiting from Italy. She immediately fell in love with him. She was sure to make him notice her. Just as their eyes met, she could see the mutual expression of love. She overheard Lacy Bennett whispering to her friend. He's not Italian, you know. The Governor just doesn't want it known his eldest daughter gave birth to a Nigra. Poor thing, he probably doesn't even know himself. No one knows what became of the Governors daughter. Its rumored she went up North.

Gracie Mae*: I vow to myself, if I cannot love this man I will not love.*

On Gracie's next trip to town she made it a point to ask Harriett if perhaps she had some things she needed delivered to anyone in town. She warned Harriett that her secret compartments on the buggy would eventually be found out.

For the next several months Gracie Mae did what she could to help Harriett get as many to freedom as she could.

The fall was also time for slaves "FIREBALL". The slaves gathered up crop remnants such as cotton, hay and whatever and wrapped them with rags into large balls. The slaves would dress in bright colorful costumes and head garb. The dancing and singing was phenomenal. Inside a large circle, the men folk gathered the balls that had been soaked in gasoline, lit them on fire and tossed them to and fro. The brilliance of the "FIREBALL" seen away as far as Africa. The smell of love and promise was like incense to Kings, Queens and all the children of the slaves' homelands. Master and all his plantation watched in amazement.

Voice*:* Everyone a seed...harvest for the world...Isleys

LATER

Gracie Mae was awakened by the chaos outside.

Gracie: Mom?

Ms. M: Gracie go back to bed.

Gracie: (*Looking out the window*) What is Father doing? What is going on?

Ms. M: Little Betty *(The cooks daughter)* was caught in a stolen ballet outfit dancing like she was a white ballet dancer. Gracie you know such mockery is not tolerated. The Nigras have gotten beside themselves. There will never be a Nigra ballerina.

Gracie: This cannot be happening!!!! I am so sorry. Little Betty!! I am so sorry!!!!!!!!

Ms. M: You better not let that mob hear you say that. You will be next. I can't protect you from that.

Little Betty was taken into the field and strung up to a tree. As the noose tightened around her neck, she began to declare...

Little Betty: You cannot kill my dream. My seed lives.

From her limp hands seeds fell to the ground. Blood pouring and running down from UNDER HER DRESS to her dangling feet splashed upon and saturated the seeds below. Her feet begin to move. Little Betty is joined by Joan Myers, Janet Collins, Raven Wilkinson, Delores Brown, and Misty Copeland. They grace us in dance like Heavenly Hosts.

The ancestors liken unto a whirlwind of leaves gather her up and carry her away.

Gracie Mae was so devastated she did not speak for weeks.

Out of guilt Ms. M tried to awaken her daughter's silence.

Ms. M.: My darling how can I make this right?

Gracie: Elnora. Go down to your husband's brother's plantation and bring Elnora home.

When Ms. Elnora returned, she was old and worn. She was happy to be home with her family.

Elnora*:* This is like Heaven.

Two days later Gracie Mae, with her journal in tow, boarded the train for UP NORTH. On the train, with much amazement she caught sight of a tall, handsome, bronzed man with curly black hair.

MONTHS LATER

Bennett delivered a note to Harriett:

Gracie Mae*:* My Beloved friend Harriett, I just want you to know that I am safe in New York. All is well for me. I miss you and your babies dearly. Please kiss

Elnora for me. The Abolitionists are very active here. I pray that they continue to be a help for you as you continue to save lives. I was told that Lorainne Despeaux moved to New York to be near her sister after her husband died. Viola is with her still making dresses. Lorainne opened a dress shop called "Dressed by

VI/SIX". Harriett I do miss you so and wish you could join me...Gracie.

Harriett: Dear Friend,

I am happy you have found happiness in your new life. My heart longs for you as well. However, my home is here on the plantation where I can do much good. I must continue my calling. The HARVEST is depending on me. There is so much work to do............................. Harriett

Ms. O.: Harriett we honor you.

As the guests are enjoying themselves, Ms. O compliments Viola D. on her beautiful gown. The two laugh while flipping up their hems. You got it "DRESSED BY VI".

THE END

Let us begin again.

There is much work to be done.

WRITTEN BY MYRA L. TURNAGE © 8/28/15

SPECIAL THANKS TO ROBERT CLAY FOR HIS CONTRIBUTION TO THE OPENING MONOLOGUE AND SCENES I, II, III, AND IV

ABOUT THE AUTHOR – *Myra L. Turnage*

For the first 17 years of her life, Myra spent most of her time in rural Mississippi. Both her parents and grandparents were born and raised in a small town less than 50 miles from Memphis. Growing up there, she experienced very little cultural versatility. Racial tension was at a minimum, probably because of segregation. Myra's interaction with people who did not look like her came when she attended High School where competition was more about popularity than race.

Myra attended college at Jackson State University where she began studying towards her nursing degree. She completed her studies at Ole Miss, Home of the Rebels. After graduating and practicing nursing in Jackson for a few months, Myra moved to Atlanta, Ga. In Atlanta, she continued her nursing career. However, her passion for writing, which she has had since grade school, seemed to overtake her interest so she began putting pen to paper. Please enjoy this story about individuals whose lives were worlds apart but were bonded by strength, love and hope.

www.ingramcontent.com/pod-product-compliance
Lightning Source LLC
Chambersburg PA
CBHW061755040426

42447CB00011B/2305